Everything You Need to Know About

PROTECTING YOURSELF AND OTHERS FROM ABDUCTION

Abduction is a serious problem in the United States, but if you take proper precautions, you can protect yourself and others from being abducted.

Everything You Need to Know About

PROTECTING YOURSELF AND OTHERS FROM ABDUCTION

Thomas Wiloch

THE ROSEN PUBLISHING GROUP, INC.
NEW YORK

Published in 1998 by The Rosen Publishing Group, Inc.
29 East 21st Street, New York, NY 10010

First Edition

Library of Congress Cataloging-in-Publication Data

Wiloch, Thomas, 1955-
    Everything you need to know about protecting yourself and others from abduction / Thomas Wiloch.—1st ed.
    p.   cm. —(The need to know library)
    Includes bibliographical references and index.
    Summary: Offers information about the problem of abduction and advice on how to protect oneself from becoming a victim of this crime.
    ISBN 0-8239-2553-6
    1. Abduction—United States—Preventive—Juvenile literature. 2. Teenagers—United States—Life skills guides—Juvenile literature. 3. Safety education—United States—Juvenile literature. [1. Kidnapping—Prevention. 2. Safety.]
I. Title. II. Series.
HV6574.U6W56   1998
613.6—dc21
                                               97-44784
                                                      CIP
                                                          AC

Manufactured in the United States of America

Contents

Introduction

Tim was walking to the ballpark when a car pulled up next to him. A man rolled down the window and asked if Tim wanted a job. The man said that he was looking for window washers for a nearby apartment building that his company was constructing. The job paid $10 an hour. Tim saw that the man was wearing overalls and a hard hat. In the backseat of his car were rolled-up blueprints and a box of tools. Tim knew there was a construction site two blocks away. And the money sounded good to him. So Tim decided to go with the man. Several weeks later, the police arrested the man who offered Tim the job. He had abducted, raped, and murdered eleven teenage boys, including Tim.

This true story shows how vulnerable children and teenagers are to abduction. Abduction, the taking of a person using physical force, threats, or tricks, is a serious and dangerous problem. According to the U.S. Justice Department, over 100,000 young people are the victims of attempted abduction each year.

Some victims of abduction are raped or molested. Other victims are found murdered, and some are never seen again.

In this book, we will discuss various safety precautions that young people can take to protect themselves and others from being abducted. In the following chapters, you will learn how to tell the difference between a safe stranger and a dangerous stranger. You will learn who abductors are, how they choose their victims, and what tricks they use to lure young people into dangerous situations. You will also learn precautions for preventing an abduction at home, while driving, in public places, and even on the Internet.

According to the Department of Justice, two-thirds of the sexual offenders in state prisons are serving time for sexually assaulting children under the age of eighteen. Ninety-seven percent of them are men. For this reason, abductors and child molesters will be referred to as "he" throughout this book.

Children and young people are the most frequent victims of abduction. For this reason, it is very important for young people to know how to protect themselves and others from being abducted.

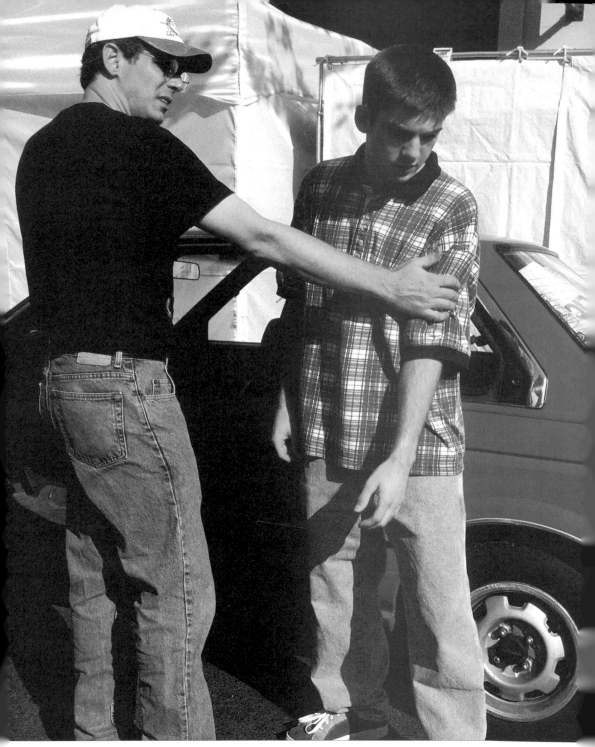

Some abductors use tricks to lure their victims into going somewhere with them, but other abductors use physical force instead.

Chapter 1

The Abduction Problem

*F*ifteen-year-old Morgan was walking home from school when a man wearing a cap and a T-shirt and carrying a clipboard came up to her. He smiled at Morgan and asked her if she wanted to enter a raffle for tickets to see an upcoming concert at the Coliseum. Morgan's favorite band was playing at the concert, but she couldn't afford the tickets. Morgan saw that the man's cap and T-shirt had the Coliseum logo on it, so she thought it was okay. But as she filled out the raffle ticket, the man grabbed her and pushed her into his car. Despite the efforts of the police, Morgan's parents, and many others, Morgan was never found.

According to the U.S. Department, about 4,000 children and teenagers are abducted by strangers every year. Of these, about 300 will be murdered by their abductors. Most of the other victims will be raped, sexually molested, or physically hurt. Sexual assault is often the primary reason for most abductions.

What is most frightening about these figures, however, is that in reality they are significantly higher. When a child is abducted and later found dead, the police often classify the crime as a murder instead of an abduction. Similarly, the crime of abduction and rape may be classified only as a rape. The actual number of abductions, then, is higher than the official numbers show. Organizations involved in protecting young people estimate that the number of young people abducted may be as high as 40,000 a year.

There are many reasons for the growing abduction problem. In the United States today, some 60,000 criminals are classified as sexual predators. They have been convicted of raping or sexually molesting children or young people. Many of these criminals are free on the streets. This is because even when they are caught, they often serve relatively short prison terms before being released. Studies show that many sexual predators, even after receiving professional therapy, will molest or rape again.

Because sexual predators pose such a danger to society, six states—Arizona, California, Kansas, Minnesota, Washington, and Wisconsin—have recently implemented laws that allow authorities to lock up such offenders indefinitely even after they have served their sentences.

Megan's Law

In 1996, the United States Congress passed a new law designed to help protect young people from sexual predators. Megan's Law orders local police officials to inform a neighborhood when a convicted child molester moves into their community. This law was named after Megan Kanka, a seven-year-old girl from New Jersey who was abducted, raped, and murdered in 1994.

Megan was killed by a neighbor who was a convicted child molester. Neither Megan, her parents, or anyone else in the neighborhood, were aware of the man's background. While Megan's Law and other laws strive to protect young people from dangerous criminals, you also need to take safety measures to protect yourself and others.

When Loved Ones Abduct Children

Every year, about 1.8 million children are reported missing in the United States. Most of these young people have simply gotten lost, are found quickly, and are returned home unharmed.

About 350,000 missing young people are abducted by a parent, grandparent, or legal guardian during a parental custody dispute. They are often taken across state lines to prevent others from finding them. Although parents who abduct their own children are breaking the law, they often don't harm their children. They often just want their children to live with them.

Runaways are often easy targets for abductors because they have no one to protect them or alert authorities that they are missing.

Runaways

Other missing young people are runaways. They leave home when family troubles become too difficult for them to handle. Most runaways return home after a few days. Runaways are especially in danger of abduction because they often live on the streets, and there is no one to protect them. They can be robbed, raped, or even murdered.

Abduction is often only the first step in a series of crimes. The abductor wants to get his victim alone. He will use force, tricks, or bribery to lure his victims to go with him. Once he gets the victim to a secluded place with no witnesses, he attacks them. Abductors usually rape or molest their victims, and some kill their victims.

As you can see, learning to protect yourself and others from abduction should be a priority. In the following chapters, we will discuss the ways that abductions happen to help you recognize situations that may be dangerous. Following simple precautions when you are in your car, at home, or shopping at the mall can keep you safe. Teach these steps to your younger siblings to help protect them.

Chapter 2

Who Is a Stranger?

When you were younger, your parents probably taught you never to talk to strangers. Parents know that talking to the wrong sort of stranger can be dangerous. But even as you grow older and think you know how to tell the difference between a safe and a dangerous stranger, you can be deceived by tricks criminals use. Even adults are sometimes fooled by a friendly personality and a nice smile.

You talk to many people every day—store clerks, mail carriers, bank tellers, and others—who are strangers to you. Talking to strangers is necessary. You cannot get through a typical day without talking to strangers. But some strangers are dangerous, and they want to harm you. How do you tell the difference between normal and dangerous strangers? How do you avoid strangers who want to harm you?

Abductors often use a friendly personality or nice smile to trick children and teens into trusting them.

How Dangerous Strangers Behave

Normal strangers often talk to you in the course of doing their jobs. For example, the bus driver will talk about the traffic. Normal strangers usually exchange a few words and then go on their way. A dangerous stranger is someone who begins talking to you for no apparent reason or asks you inappropriate or personal questions. He may ask if you are alone, ask for your name, or ask where you live. He may ask you to help him carry his groceries or to help find his lost pet. He may ask you to go somewhere with him. Normal strangers will not do this. A normal stranger will not try to engage you in a lengthy or personal conversation. A normal stranger will not try to talk you into going somewhere with him.

A dangerous stranger will often look around while he is talking as if he doesn't want to be seen talking to you. A stranger who is worried about someone seeing the two of you together should be a warning sign that he may be a dangerous stranger.

How to Spot a Dangerous Stranger

Small children and some teenagers, and even some adults, mistakenly believe that they can tell whether a stranger is dangerous, just by the way he looks. Some people think that strangers will look dirty or dangerous, but we need to realize that a dangerous stranger will probably look like everyone else. A smile or a friendly face is not enough to make a stranger into a friend. A person's behavior is what makes him dangerous, not his appearance.

Danger Signals Children Should Know

Young children often think that if someone knows their name that person is not a stranger but a friend. Abductors know this and will try to trick a small child into telling his or her name. The abductor will call the child by the wrong name to get the child to say his or her correct name. The abductor may also read the name off a name tag on the child's clothing or overhear someone else say it. The child will naturally think that because he knows my name, he is not a stranger but a friend. Younger children need to be aware that just because someone knows their name, doesn't mean he should be trusted.

It's hard to tell the difference between normal strangers and dangerous strangers just by looking at them. Dangerous strangers often look like everyone else.

Danger Signals Teens Should Be Aware Of

You should be aware that friendly strangers may be the most dangerous. Most women who are raped in the United States are between the ages of twelve and twenty-five. They are young single women who are dating and meeting young single men. They are likely to talk with a stranger if he is good-looking and seems friendly. Many are fooled by a handsome, smiling man who seems to be flirting with them. They are flattered by his attention.

You need to be aware that a dangerous stranger may not look dangerous. Remember that a person's behavior is what makes him dangerous, not his physical appearance.

Any stranger who wants to be alone with you, who offers you a ride in his car, or who invites you to his house—no matter how friendly he seems—may be a threat to your safety.

Accepting Gifts from Strangers

Just as small children should not accept candy from strangers, teenagers must not accept gifts from strangers. These gifts may be alcohol, drugs, or pornography. It may be money to play games at an arcade or to buy clothes at the mall. A potential abductor will offer whatever gift he thinks his victim will like.

Any stranger who tries to talk you into going somewhere with him is a potential abductor. In any situation with a stranger, be aware of what he is trying to do with his conversation. Ask yourself if he wants you, for any reason, to go with him where the two of you would be alone. If you think that is his intention, get away from him quickly. He is trying to abduct you with a trick.

Chapter 3

Abductors and How They Operate

According to police sources, most abductors are pedophiles—adults who engage in sexual activities with children or young people. Pedophiles are also called child molesters. Having sex with children or with young people under the age of eighteen is illegal in the United States and throughout much of the world. Any adult who has sex with a young person is breaking the law.

Often pedophiles were sexually abused themselves as children. As they grew up, they may have started to molest children in their own families or among their circle of friends. Some pedophiles go on to molest children and teenagers they do not know, abducting them off the street or from public places. They often will abduct, molest, and then release a child. Child molesters prey upon both boys and girls.

Child Pornography

Child pornography is another common motive for abduction. Some pedophiles abduct children to take pictures of them or to videotape them in sexual situations. Child pornography is illegal in the United States and in many other countries. However, there is an underground market for such material among pedophiles throughout the world.

According to the U.S. Department of Justice, there are 250,000 to 500,000 pedophiles living in the United States. Statistics show that even those pedophiles who have been caught, jailed, and treated will probably return to child molesting once they are released from prison. Young people need to be aware of the real dangers posed by pedophiles and take steps to protect themselves.

While most abductors are child molesters, there are other criminals who abduct their victims. A rapist often abducts his victim and takes him or her to a secluded place where there will be no witnesses to the attack. Many serial killers abduct their victims before murdering them. Abduction is often the first step in a series of crimes. Protecting yourself from abduction will protect you from other crimes as well.

Common Tricks Abductors Use

One of serial killer Ted Bundy's favorite tricks was to walk with crutches. To unsuspecting victims, Bundy appeared to have a broken leg. He would ask young women in a store parking lot to help him carry groceries to his car. He seemed nice, he smiled, and he looked like he had a broken leg. Many women helped him carry his groceries. But when they reached his car, Bundy would force the woman inside and drive away. He killed at least thirty-five young women before he was caught by police and eventually executed.

Sometimes abductors use force instead of a ruse to trap their victim. They drag the victim into a van or a wooded area. Then they threaten the victim with a weapon, such as a gun or a knife.

Part of protecting yourself and others against abduction involves knowing what tricks abductors usually use, who they usually abduct, and where they usually find their victims. Abductors have been using the same kinds of tricks, looking for the same kinds of victims, and abducting their victims in the same kinds of places for many years. Knowing how abductors operate can save you from becoming an abductor's next victim.

Asking for Help

One trick abductors use is to ask a young person for help. The abductor may ask for directions, or for help with his car door because his arms are loaded down with packages. You should be suspicious of any stranger who asks for your help. When adults need help, they turn to other adults, not young people they do not know. Any stranger who asks for your help should be avoided.

Sometimes abductors will use a trick to get close to their victims, such as pretending to be lost and asking for directions.

Bribery

Another trick used by abductors is bribery. When you were younger, your parents and teachers probably taught you not to take candy or gifts from strangers. They know that abductors often use candy or other treats as a bribe to convince children that the abductor is a friend. Abductors might bribe teenagers with drugs or alcohol or the chance to play a new computer game. Remember that a stranger who offers you something of value may be trying to trick you. He may be trying to coax you into going somewhere alone with him.

Some teenagers have been abducted by strangers who offered them jobs. Abductors know that a well-paying job is hard for some teens to turn down. Remember that real employers do not stop people in the street and offer them work. Real employers run newspaper ads or go through employment agencies to find employees.

Any stranger who offers you a job or anything else is acting in a suspicious manner. Keep in mind that if someone approaches you on the street and offers you something that sounds too good to be true, it probably is. You don't know the person, and he doesn't know you, so why would he do you such a favor? Ask yourself what other motives he might have. Don't be fooled by a bribe.

There's Trouble at Home

One of the most common tricks used by abductors is to make up a fake story about a family emergency. This trick is often used on small children, but it's sometimes used on teenagers too.

A stranger will approach a young person walking home from school. He may say "Your mom's been in an accident, and she asked me to take you to the hospital right away." Another example might be, "I know your dad from work. He can't pick you up, so he sent me instead." It is important that small children know immediately that such stories sound wrong and that their parents would never send a stranger to drive them anywhere. They should never believe any story a stranger tells them about an illness or an accident in the family.

If there has been an emergency, your family will get in touch with you. They will not send a stranger.

Beware of any stranger who offers you something that sounds too good to be true. It may be a trick to lure you into going somewhere with him.

Code Words

Child-protection experts recommend that parents or guardians arrange a secret code or password with their children. If someone approaches you on the streets and tells you that your parents sent him, ask the person for the password. If the person doesn't know it, then you will know that your parents didn't send him. And you should get away from this person as quickly as possible.

Impersonators

Some abductors will pretend to be a police officer, a minister, or another official person. Few children will think there is any danger in getting into a car with a police officer who has shown them a badge. Older children may be tricked by persons pretending to be truant officers or school officials. Teenagers may think it is safe to help a man wearing a clerical collar find his lost keys. But keep in mind that a stranger wearing a uniform is still a stranger. Unless there is a good reason to think that someone is a real police officer or minister or other authority figure, it is safer to stay away. Look for clues before getting involved with them. A man wearing a police uniform who steps out of a patrol car is probably a real police officer. A man who only shows you a badge may not be.

Also, ask yourself if what the person is asking you to do falls under his job description. A real police officer wouldn't ask you to get into his car without a legitimate reason. A real minister wouldn't come up to a young person on the street and ask for help to find his lost keys. Examine the situation and use your judgement. If you don't trust the person or what he says, or something doesn't feel right, don't get involved with him.

When Abductors Use Force

Although most abductors trick their victims into going with them, some will use force or threats instead. These abductors will threaten the victim with a weapon, such as a knife or a gun. They may simply grab the person and pull him or her into a car or van. This kind of abduction will usually take place in a secluded area. Abductors do not want witnesses to their crime. They do not want anyone to hear their victim's cries for help.

To prevent forcible abduction, do not go into secluded places alone. Alleys, abandoned houses, wooded areas, and similar places are dangerous. These are all places where you cannot be seen or heard by other people. You could be attacked by a stranger without anyone else knowing. If you called for help, no one would hear you. Avoiding secluded places and staying in sight of other people when you are out in public make you safer from abduction.

A Confident Attitude

Forcible abduction can also be prevented by a strong, confident attitude. Abductors often choose victims who look like easy targets. They want someone who will go along with them quietly without resistance. If you are alert in public, keeping aware of who is nearby and what they are doing, you are a harder target for abductors. If you seem confused, lost, or distracted, you make an easier target. Looking down at the ground as you walk or wearing headphones make it easier for someone to take you by surprise.

Convicted serial killers have told police that they chose their victims based on how they behaved in public. They have said that alert persons were too difficult to take by surprise, but inattentive people made easy targets. If you stay aware of your surroundings whenever you are in a public place, you greatly lessen your chances of being abducted.

If someone does try to abduct you by force, remember that he does not want to attract attention to himself.

A confident attitude is sometimes your best defense against abductors.

Anything you can do to attract the attention of other people will make him want to leave you alone. Small children who were helpless in fighting off their abductors have screamed so loudly that it caught the attention of nearby persons who came and stopped the abduction.

Abductors want easy targets. If you make noise, you become a difficult target. You may attract the help of people nearby. Shouting for help or making any sort of loud noise can scare an abductor away.

Although adults are also abducted, most victims of abduction are young people. Most abductions happen in public places, such as parking lots, playgrounds, on the street, or in shopping malls. But some abductions also take place at the victim's home. The following chapters will discuss how abductors operate in all these locations and how you can avoid becoming a victim.

Chapter 4

Safety at Home

Sarah was home alone washing dishes. The door-bell rang. She looked through the window and saw a man standing on the porch. He was wearing a postal work-er's uniform and held a package in one hand and a clip-board in the other. Sarah opened the door but kept the chain on. "I have a package for you," the man told her. "You have to sign for it." Sarah undid the chain and opened the door. The man handed her a pen and the clipboard. While Sarah was signing her name, the man pushed his way into the house. He forced her out the back door and into the alley where his car was parked. He drove Sarah to an empty stretch of road and raped her.

Strangers at the Door

Every day, criminals pretending to be deliverymen or repairmen trick people into letting them into their

Don't open your door to strangers. Abductors sometimes
pretend to be deliverymen to trick you into opening your door.

homes. Once inside, they abduct, rob, rape, and murder innocent people. Other criminals pretend to be from the water department and want to "read the meter." Sometimes they pretend to be maintenance men or painters, plumbers, or building inspectors. Criminals have found that pretending to be deliverymen or repairmen is a useful trick for getting inside a house.

Many of these crimes can be prevented with simple precautions. If someone claims to be from the post office, or from a mail delivery company, look at the uniform. Does the jacket match the trousers? Do the shoes match the uniform? Many times, the criminal has stolen only part of a full uniform, and the rest of his clothes do not match. Is there a mail truck or delivery truck parked nearby? Real postal employees delivering packages will do so in a truck. They will not walk door-to-door with an armload of packages. Look at the package too. Is it addressed to you? Does it have a return address from someone you recognize? Are you expecting a package?

If you have any doubts about a postal employee at the door, just ask that he leave the package outside, or tell him that you will pick it up at the post office later. It is better to go through some extra trouble over a package than to put yourself at risk from a stranger.

Repairmen who come to the door must also be checked carefully. If you are not expecting a repairman to come to your house, do not let him in. Real repairmen do not arrive unannounced. And they usually don't show up at all unless you've asked them to come. If you have asked for a repairman, check his ID or call his office before you let him in. See whether he has come in a marked company truck or van.

Fake repairmen may offer to give your furnace a free inspection. They may say that your neighbors have been having phone problems and they want to check your phone too. You should be suspicious of any story a stranger at the door tells you. Just because a stranger is wearing a work uniform and carrying tools does not mean he is a real repairman.

Some abductors simply follow their victims home and force their way in when the victims have opened their front door. To prevent this, have your keys out and ready. Check that no one is behind you before opening your door.

If you are driven home, have the person wait until you are safely inside your home. When returning from a friend's house, always have them call to make sure you got home safely

May I Use Your Phone?

One of the most popular tricks that criminals use to enter homes is to ask if they can use the telephone. People of all ages have been victimized by criminals who asked to use the phone, came in, and then attacked or robbed them. The criminal who uses this trick plays on our natural desire to be polite and helpful. When a stranger says, "My car has broken down. May I use your phone to call a tow truck?" it is easy to say yes. But knowing about this trick can prevent you from falling for it.

One good way to protect yourself from a potential abductor is to tell the person that you will make the phone call for him. If the stranger claims that there has been a car accident, offer to call the police. If the stranger needs a tow truck, offer to call for one. If someone is sick or hurt, offer to call an ambulance. Offering to make the call yourself—while the stranger waits outside—will defeat the trick. If there is a real problem and the stranger is telling the truth, you will help out by making the phone call for him. If it is a trick, however, you will keep the criminal from getting inside your house.

Baby-Sitting

Many teenagers baby-sit either someone else's children, or younger siblings. Baby-sitting is an important and serious job. During the time that you are baby-sitting a child, you are responsible for his or her safety and well-being. A baby-sitter temporarily assumes the role of a parent to the children he or she is caring for.

When you agree to baby-sit someone else's children, you must take the job seriously. Find out the names and ages of the children, their bedtimes, what foods they can eat, and what medicines they may need to take while you are there. Ask who the children may play with, where the children may play, and who may visit while the parents are gone. Get the phone number and address of where the parents will be. Also, make sure that you have emergency phone numbers handy for the police, fire department, and the nearest hospital.

Baby-sitting is a serious job. The safety of the children in your care is your responsibility.

Lock the doors immediately after the parents leave. Many simple home crimes begin with a thief or attacker walking through an unlocked door. Do not let anyone into the house who has not been approved by the parents beforehand. If someone who has not been approved comes to the door, tell them that you will deliver a message for them. Never allow the children to answer the door. Your own friends should not visit when you are baby-sitting. The children are in your care, not your friends'. Also, having your friends there can distract you from taking proper care of the children.

If the phone rings, do not tell the caller that you are home alone with the children. Tell the caller the parents are unavailable at the moment and take a message.

If the parents have told you that the children can play in the yard, watch the children closely when they are outside. Stay nearby to make sure they do not wander off. Be aware of anyone who is hanging around or trying to talk to you or the children. If a situation or person makes you feel uncomfortable, take the children inside immediately, lock the door, and call the police.

If you are baby-sitting at night, do not allow the children to go outside. If you hear strange noises or detect odd activity, don't go outside yourself. Instead, switch on the outside lights and call the police immediately.

You should also follow the tips discussed earlier about opening the door to strangers. Remember, someone who is wearing a uniform or asking to use the phone may be dangerous.

Baby-sitting can be a rewarding job. It can give you an increased sense of responsibility while earning you extra money. But baby-sitting is also a serious job because the children you baby-sit depend on you for protection. A good baby-sitter takes precautions to ensure that the children in his or her care are safe.

Taking safety precautions is especially important in the home. If an abductor gets inside your home, you will be in a confined space, where your cries for help will not be heard. Don't open your door to any stranger —no matter what story he tells you.

Chapter 5

Safety While Driving

*P*aul *was driving to the store with his friend Jane. They stopped at a red light. While they waited for the light to change, Paul and Jane listened to the radio and talked about what they wanted to buy at the store. Suddenly, the car door was pulled open by a man with a gun. "Move over," the man ordered Paul, and he climbed in behind the steering wheel. The man drove off at a high speed. A few minutes later, the man pulled the car into an alley and ordered Paul and Jane to hand over their money and jewelry. "Now get out," he said, waving the gun at them. Paul and Jane quickly got out of the car, and the man sped away.*

Carjacking

Paul and Jane were lucky that they were not hurt by the carjacker who abducted and robbed them. Carjacking,

Carjacking is a growing problem. Victims have been robbed, hurt, and even killed by carjackers.

the theft of a car through the use of force or threats against the driver, is a growing problem in the United States. It is a serious crime in which the victim can be robbed, hurt, raped, and even killed. Each year about 300 people are abducted during carjackings.

A carjacking can happen when the driver is getting into or out of his or her car. It can also happen when a car is stopped at a red light or stop sign. Carjacking is a dangerous crime because carjackers often threaten the driver and passengers with a weapon. Sometimes, the carjacker will force the driver and passengers out of the car so he can steal it. Sometimes, he will drive away with the driver and passengers so he can rob or harm them.

Safety Precautions

You can protect yourself from carjacking by following a few simple rules. When returning to your parked car, look for strangers loitering nearby. If someone is loitering near your parked car, walk past it. Come back when the stranger has left. When you do approach your car, have your keys ready. Fumbling with your keys only gives a carjacker time to get close to you. Before getting into a parked car, check that no one is hiding in the backseat or on the floor.

While driving your car, keep the doors locked and windows shut. This prevents anyone from getting inside. Beware of people approaching your car when you are stopped at a red light or stop sign. If someone suspicious approaches your car, drive away at a safe speed. Some carjackers pretend that they want to ask you directions or sell you something so they can get close enough to open your car door.

If another car bumps yours while you are driving, do not get out of the car. Signal the other driver to follow you. Then drive to the nearest police station or a busy, well-lit store, restaurant, or gas station. You can exchange insurance information there. Some carjackers purposely cause minor accidents in secluded areas in order to lure drivers from their cars.

Never stop and offer assistance to stranded motorists. Carjackers sometimes pretend that their cars have broken down to lure other motorists into getting out of their cars.

Since most carjackings occur between 10 PM and 2 AM, you should always try to avoid driving late at night. Avoid driving in dangerous neighborhoods if there is another route available. Also, avoid driving through areas you're unfamiliar with. When you are lost, you become an easy target. Carjacking is preventable if you take the proper steps to avoid it.

Car Breakdowns

If your car breaks down or runs out of gas on the highway, you are vulnerable to criminals. Many stranded motorists have been attacked or robbed by strangers after their cars have broken down. These strangers will offer to help repair the car or drive the motorist to a gas station. But these offers are tricks to get the motorist out of the car which makes it easier for the motorist to be robbed or harmed.

Car breakdowns can often be prevented. Make sure that your car has enough gasoline before leaving on any trip, no matter how close the destination may be. Keep the car in good repair so that the chances of it breaking down are small.

But sometimes even the most reliable car will break down for some reason. If your car does break down on the highway, stay inside, lock the doors, and shut the windows. Wait until a police car comes by and flag it down. If another motorist stops and offers to help, open the window just far enough to ask him to call a tow truck for you. Do not get out of the car, even if he claims he can fix your problem.

When you hitchhike, you make yourself vulnerable to abductors and other dangerous strangers.

Always keep a list of emergency numbers in the car. It is also helpful to have a cell phone. Look into buying or subscribing to a cell phone service that offers emergency calls only. This type of service is usually cheaper than paying for unlimited usage. If you get into trouble, you can call your parents or a tow truck without leaving your car. And you will not have to wait for a police car to come by.

If you get lost, don't drive around aimlessly; this makes you an easier target. Drive to a busy place to use your phone. If you don't have a cell phone, use a phone inside a store. If you get out of your car to ask for directions or to use the phone, always lock your doors, no matter how brief you think your call or conversation may be.

Hitchhiking

Some teenagers think that hitchhiking is an adventurous, thrilling thing to do or an easy way to get around. But countless crimes have been committed against hitchhikers by the motorists who have picked them up. Hitchhiking can be dangerous to both the hitchhiker and the motorist. Hitchhiking is a very dangerous activity that has led to the murder, rape, and robbery of many teenagers.

Hitchhiking is dangerous because it puts you in a car alone with a stranger. You are entrusting your life to someone you don't know. This person could be a rapist or a thief or even a killer. And the stranger is driving the car and can take you wherever he wants to go. The danger is the same whether someone picks you up or you pick someone else up.

Simply put, hitchhiking is too dangerous a way to get around. If you cannot drive or get a ride, take a bus or subway or walk. All these methods of transportation are safer than hitchhiking.

Chapter 6

Safety in Public Places

Whenever you are in a public place, you are a potential crime victim. In public places, such as shopping malls or a baseball stadium, we meet and mingle with many strangers. Criminals look for victims wherever people normally gather.

Being careful in any public place means being aware of the people around you and what they are doing. You can avoid being the victim of a crime by avoiding the people and situations that may be dangerous to you.

Parking Lots

Many crimes occur in the parking lots of stores and office buildings. Because of the many vehicles parked there, it is often hard to spot a criminal in a parking lot. He can crouch between parked cars or hide behind a parked van. He can even wait in his own car for someone to approach.

Criminals have stolen cars, robbed, raped, abducted, and even murdered people in parking lots.

To protect yourself in a parking lot, follow many of the same rules you follow in other situations. Be on the lookout for strangers who may be hanging around. Don't walk where you cannot easily be seen by others, such as behind a parked truck or van.

In addition to these rules, there are special rules to follow in a parking lot. At night, park under a street-light. Park as close as you can to the store or building you are going to visit. Park so that your door is not next to a van or truck. When you get out of the car, it is easy for someone in a van to grab you and pull you inside without anyone else noticing.

Before you get out of your car, look around to see if there is anyone suspicious nearby. Do not get out if there is. Drive to another parking space if you do not feel safe where you are.

When you get out of your car, unlock only the door you are using. Rapists and thieves sometimes jump into a car through the passenger side when the doors are unlocked.

When you walk from your car to the store, do not walk too close to other parked cars. Criminals can easily hide between parked cars, especially at night. Walk in the middle of the lane, keeping as much space as possible between you and the cars.

When you return to your car, have your keys in your hand, ready to open the door. If you see a suspicious

Always have your keys out, ready to open your door, and be aware of anyone loitering near your car.

person hanging around your car, walk back to the store and report him to the security guard.

Before getting into your parked car, check that no one is hiding in the backseat or on the floor.

If you are carrying packages from the store, take them inside the car with you. Do not stop to put them in the trunk. When you put packages in the trunk, you turn your back to people approaching, which makes it easy for someone to sneak up on you. If you have a large package, have a store employee help you carry it to your car or drive to the store entrance and load it into the trunk there.

If you are shopping in a mall, ask a security guard to walk you to your car. Many malls have such courtesy patrol. It is best to finish your shopping before most of the other shoppers leave. Abductors are less likely to do anything when there are people around.

In the Store

Child molesters often go to stores to find young children. A molester looks for a child who is lost or whose parent or older brother or sister is not paying attention. The molester will then try to take the child from the store. Sometimes, he will tell the child a fake story to try to trick him or her into leaving. Other times, he will simply grab the child and drag him or her out of the store. Even if the child cries, most people won't think he or she is being abducted. They may think that the child has misbehaved and is being punished or that the child is crying because he or she is not feeling well.

Protecting Younger Siblings

Teach your younger brothers and sisters that if they get lost at a store, they should not wander around looking for their parents. They should not leave the store. They should go to a store clerk at the cash register or to a uniformed security guard at the door. Going to a mother or father with children is also safe. The child should say that he or she is lost and needs help.

You can protect your younger brothers and sisters by watching them carefully when you are in a store together. Small children often get bored while their parents or older brothers and sisters are shopping. They are easily distracted by the merchandise on display or by playing a game of hide-and-seek to pass the time. When you are shopping, make sure that your younger brothers and sisters stay close by.

A good way to do this is to involve them in the shopping process. Ask them to help find the items you want to buy. As you walk along a store aisle, they can point and show you the item when they see it. Ask them what color or style they like best. Involving children in your shopping keeps them from getting distracted and separated from you.

Dawn was walking home from school when she noticed a van driving slowly behind her. She saw two men in the van watching her. Dawn moved away from the curb and began walking faster. The van sped up. Suddenly, a man jumped out and started running after Dawn. Dawn screamed for help and headed for a nearby store where she saw a group of people. The man quickly got back into the van, and it drove away. A neighbor who had ran out of his house when he heard Dawn's scream took down the van's license plate number. That information and Dawn's description of the two men helped the police to track down the two suspects. They were arrested by police for attempted abduction later that evening. The police investigation discovered that the two men had been abducting and raping young women like Dawn.

Walking Down the Street

When you walk on the street, there are certain precautions you can take to keep yourself safe from abduction. If possible, do not walk alone. Have a friend walk with you. Avoid walking after dark. If you do have to walk in the dark, walk only in well-lit areas. Keep away from shadowy walkways or places hidden by overgrown shrubbery. These are places where an attacker can hide. Keep yourself in view of others as much as possible. Do not take shortcuts through wooded areas or down alleys. These are isolated places where a crime can easily be committed against you without any witnesses.

If you notice someone following you on foot, cross the street or walk to a building or group of people. If the person following you is persistent, go into a store or gas station and ask the clerk to call the police. If a car follows you, walk in the opposite direction from the way the car is driving. This makes it harder for you to be followed. If someone gets out of the car and comes toward you, run into a store or other public place or toward a group of people. If you need to, scream to attract the attention of others in the area.

If the attacker drives away, try to get his license plate number or try to remember what he looks like or what he was wearing. Report it immediately to the police. You may save someone else from being abducted. Abductors often try several possible victims before finding one they can easily attack.

One way to protect yourself on the streets is to always walk
with a friend.

Jogging and Bicycling

Many young people enjoy jogging or bicycling for exercise or recreation. While these activities can be healthy and fun, they can also be potentially dangerous, so always take precautions. Police statistics show that several thousand rapes, beatings, and murders are committed against joggers or cyclists every year in the United States.

Many attacks on joggers or cyclists take place in isolated areas of parks or on scenic wooded trails where few people are around. In 1989, a woman jogging in Central Park in New York City was forcibly dragged into a grove of trees. She was gang raped, beaten, and left for dead. This crime shocked the whole country. The woman was jogging in a quiet, empty section of the park when the attack occurred. Fortunately, she survived the vicious attack. But many women joggers have been murdered in similar attacks in quiet parks.

It is safer to jog where you can always see and be seen by other people. Busy streets or crowded public parks with many pedestrians are the safest places for jogging or cycling.

Joggers should not run alone. Criminals often see a lone woman as a much easier target. It is much safer to run with a friend or two. Even running with a pet dog will increase your level of safety.

Always jog or cycle in the daytime. During daylight hours, criminals have less of a chance to attack or abduct you without being seen. If you have to run or cycle in the evening, do it in well-lit, well-populated areas.

If a car or van approaches while you are jogging or bicycling, move away from the street. Be especially suspicious of vans, because you can be quickly pulled inside and out of sight. If the vehicle slows down or pulls up alongside you, run or cycle in the opposite direction from the way it is headed. Go to the nearest populated place—an office building or a gas station—and call the police. Try to give a description of the car or van, the driver, and the license plate number. This will help the police track him down faster.

Many joggers and cyclists carry a small hand-held alarm to sound if they get into trouble. A loud noise will always draw attention to you, and no criminal wants to attract attention. Others carry defense sprays, such as Mace or pepper spray. Think carefully before buying one, however, because often attackers can take it away and use it on their victims. However, these products should only be used as last resorts. The best option is to never place yourself in a potentially dangerous situation where you could be harmed. This means always taking precautions and staying alert.

Public Telephones

Some criminals prey upon people using public telephones because the victim is turned away from the street and cannot see them approach. The victim's hands are busy holding the phone, fumbling with coins, and dialing the number. Many abductions that end with murder or rape have occurred at pay telephones. Almost

When using a public phone, always turn around and face the street. This makes it harder for an attacker to take you by surprise.

30,000 crimes a year happen while the victim is using a pay telephone.

To reduce the risk of abduction while using a pay telephone, use the following precautions:

- Choose a phone located in a populated area, and be sure it can be seen from the street.
- Make sure that there are no parked trucks or vans blocking your view.
- Look around while you insert coins and dial the number.
- Face the street while you are talking on the phone. This will allow you to see who is nearby and make it harder for an attacker to take you by surprise.

Be suspicious of anyone who approaches you, even if they are asking for change or for directions. Do not engage in conversation with them. If a car or van slowly approaches while you are on the phone, immediately move away and head toward the nearest populated area.

Chapter 7

Safety on the Internet

Today an ever increasing number of teenagers are logging on to the Internet. Many teens turn to the Internet for help with homework or school projects, or to play games or talk with others about common interests. It is important for teens to know that molesters and abductors also log on to the Internet looking for victims. Teenagers are especially at risk because they are more likely to participate in online discussions about relationships and sexual activity.

There are teens who have been molested by people they met over the Internet. A thirty-year-old abductor or child molester may log on to the Internet and pretend to be a teenager himself. This way, he can trick teens into trusting him. Take the following safety precautions when logging on to the Internet:

- Never give out any personal information, such as your home address, telephone number, or school name, and never send someone your picture.

• If you are going to meet someone, make sure that
  the meeting place is in a public area with many
  people around. Take someone else with you, and
  let your parents or friends know about the meeting. Never agree to a meeting at the stranger's
  home or your own home, or in a secluded spot.
• Be careful about claims that sound too good to be
  true. Offers of jobs or free products should be a
  warning signal, especially if it involves going to
  someone's home.
• Keep in mind that no matter how friendly or nice
  a person may seem—or what he tells you about
  himself—he may not be telling the truth. You can't
  hear or see him, and you really don't know him, so
  there's no reason to trust him.

The Internet can be a fun and exciting way to learn
new things and meet new people. Most of the people
you meet may be there for the same reasons, and most
of them mean you no harm. But you need to keep in
mind that there are individuals who have other inten-
tions. Always use safety precautions to keep yourself
and others safe.

Abduction is a serious problem that has taken the
lives of many young people. Sometimes, abducted children are molested and then released. These children
and their families and friends are sometimes able to
heal and return to normal lives. But more often than

not, the experience will have lasting, often devastating, effects on the rest of their lives. For the families, friends, and communities of children who are killed or never heard from again, their pain will never end.

You can help protect yourself, your friends, and your siblings from abduction by taking the necessary precautions with your friends and with children you know. The more young people know about the crime of abduction and how to protect themselves, the better their chances are of not becoming a victim.

Glossary

bribery   Favors or gifts given to a person to influence his or her decision.

carjacking   The theft of a car using force or threats against the driver.

hitchhiking   Going from place to place by getting free rides from passing cars.

impersonator   A person pretending to be someone else.

indefinitely No time limit.

loitering   Staying in an area for no obvious reason.

molest   To physically force sexual advances upon another.

pedophile   Adults who engage in sexual activities with children or teenagers.

pornography Materials, such as books or videos, that show sexual activity to excite the viewer sexually.

rapist   A person who has sex with someone without his or her consent, often through the use of threats or force.

recreation   Play or amusement.

ruse   A trick.

serial killer   A person who kills several people using
similar patterns or methods over a period of time.

sexual predator   A person who attacks others,
usually to rape or molest them.

truant officer   An official who is responsible for
bringing kids back to school when they are out of
school without permission.

vulnerable   Open to attack or injury.

For Further Reading

Chaiet, Donna. *Staying Safe on the Streets*. New York: The Rosen Publishing Group, 1995.

————. *Staying Safe at Home*. New York: The Rosen Publishing Group, 1995.

————. *Staying Safe While Traveling*. New York: The Rosen Publishing Group, 1995.

DePasquale, Michael, Jr. *Streetwise Safety for Women*. Rutland, VT: Charles E. Tuttle, 1994.

Gutman, Bill. *Be Aware of Danger*. New York: Twenty-First Century Books. 1996.

Kraizer, Sherryll. *The Safe Child Book: A Common Sense Approach to Protecting Children and Teaching Children to Protect Themselves*. New York: Fireside Books, 1996.

Marshall, W. L., D. R. Laws, and H. E. Barbaree. *Handbook of Sexual Assault*. New York: Plenum Press, 1990.

Mizell, Louis, Jr. *Street Sense for Women: How to Stay Safe in a Violent World*. New York: Berkley Books, 1993.

Stuber, Robert. *Missing! Stranger Abduction: Smart Strategies to Keep Your Child Safe.* Kansas City: Andrews & McMeel, 1996.

Thomas, Matt, Denise Loveday and Larry Strauss. *Defend Yourself! Every Woman's Guide to Safeguarding Her Life.* New York: Avon Books, 1995.

Contact the National Center for Missing and Exploited Children for more reading materials.

Where to Go for Help

Adam Walsh Children's Fund
9176 Alternate A-1-A, Suite 200
Lake Park, FL 33403-1445
(407) 863-7900

Child Search: National Missing Children Center
P.O. Box 73725
Houston, TX 77273
(800) 832-3773

Commission on Missing and Exploited Children
616 Adams Ave., Room 104
Memphis, TN 38105
(901) 528-8441

Heidi Search Center
2402 Pat Booker Road
Universal City, TX 78148-3210
(800) 880-3463

Missing Youth Foundation
P.O. Box 44172
Omaha, NE 68144
(800) 45-FOUND

National Center for Missing and Exploited Children
    (NCMEC)
2101 Wilson Bld., Suite 550
Arlington, VA 22201-3052
Hot line (800) THE-LOST
Web site: http://www.missingkids.com

Vanished Children's Alliance
2095 Park Ave., Suite 200
San Jose, CA 95126
(800) VANISHED
Web site: http://www.vca.org

In Canada

Missing Children Society of Canada
3501 23rd St. NE, Suite 219
Calgary, Alberto T2E 8V6

National Missing Children's Locate Center Canada Inc.
141 Holland Ave.
Ottawa, Ontario K1Y 0Y2
(613) 729-7678
Web site: http://www.childcyberspace.org

Index

About the Author

Thomas Wiloch is a freelance writer. His work has appeared in some 300 magazines, including *Publishers Weekly* and *Bloomsbury Review*. His previous books include *Mr. Templeton's Toyshop* (1995) and *Tales of Lord Shantih* (1989).

Mr. Wiloch lives in suburban Detroit with his wife, Denise.

Photo Credits

Photo on p. 12 by Michael Brandt; p. 45 by Kim Sonsky; Cover and all other photos by Ira Fox.